About the author

Glen Oglaza is an award-winning television news reporter and political correspondent with more than twenty-five years' experience with *ITN* and *Sky News*.

At *ITN*, he covered many of the biggest stories of the 1980s and 1990s, including Lockerbie, Hillsborough, the First Gulf War and the war in former Yugoslavia. He was part of the award-winning ITN teams covering the fall of the Berlin Wall, the plight of the Kurds in the wake of the First Gulf War, and the massacre in Dunblane. He was BAFTA-nominated for his coverage of the London Poll Tax Riot. As a political correspondent for Sky News, he covered the premierships of Tony Blair, Gordon Brown and David Cameron from Westminster and covering many summits and bilaterals. He has worked in nearly forty countries. For many years, he has also worked with the British Army, Royal Navy and Royal Air Force, and for NATO.

Spam and Other Poems

Glen Oglaza

Spam and Other Poems

Vanguard Press

VANGUARD PAPERBACK

© Copyright 2024
Glen Oglaza

The right of Glen Oglaza to be identified as author of
this work has been asserted by him in accordance with the
Copyright, Designs and Patents Act 1988.

All Rights Reserved

No reproduction, copy or transmission of this publication
may be made without written permission.
No paragraph of this publication may be reproduced,
copied or transmitted save with the written permission of the publisher, or in
accordance with the provisions
of the Copyright Act 1956 (as amended).

Any person who commits any unauthorised act in relation to this publication
may be liable to criminal prosecution and civil claims for damages.

A CIP catalogue record for this title is available from the British Library.

ISBN 978-1-83794-361-6

This is a work of fiction. Names, characters, businesses, places, events and
incidents are either the products of the author's imagination or used in a
fictitious manner. Any resemblance to actual persons, living or dead, or actual
events is purely coincidental.

Vanguard Press is an imprint of
Pegasus Elliot Mackenzie Publishers Ltd.
www.pegasuspublishers.com

First Published in 2024

Vanguard Press
Sheraton House Castle Park
Cambridge England

Printed & Bound in Great Britain

Dedication

For Maddie and Seb

Contents

1. Most of All 13
2. Loneliness 14
3. I Confess 16
4. The Little Kick 17
5. My Loss 19
6. Things I Like 21
7. Gratitude 23
8. Millie 24
9. Birth of My First Child 26
10. My Second Child 27
11. The Lament of Growing Older 28
12. Grey 29
13. To a Teenage Son 30
14. Blond 31
15. Trumpety Trump (With Apologies to Nellie) 32
16. Spam 33
17. They Shall Not Grow Old 36
18. My Girl 38
19. Tonight 40
20. Great Ball of Fire 42
21. She 44
22. Loss 45

23. Actions Not Words 46
24. I Love You More than Anyone 47
25. Mad Vlad 4 48
26. What It Takes 49
27. The Soundtrack of My Life 50
28. She Is Gone (12 January 2023) 51
29. Rivers 53
30. Another Year 54
31. Divorce 56
32. Two Degrees 58
33. Action Now! 59
34. By Sunlight 61
35. My Trouble 'n' Strife 62
36. The Decision 64
37. Khovanskoye 66
38. The Lady in the Lake 67
39. Holidays 68
40. Maybe 69
41. My Friend's Wife 70
42. Peering through the Tears 71
43. Attention Span of This Generation 73
44. Humans 75
45. New Love 77
46. To My Ex 78

47. Larry 80
48. A Homily 82
49. Red Red lights (To the Tune of Red Red Wine) 84
50. The Whether Fourcast 86
51. The End? 87
52. At the Supermarket 89
53. Growing Old 92
54. The Funeral 94
55. Never Mind 96
56. I Bought Them a Puppy 98
57. Mad Vlad 5 100
58. Hey Kids! 102
59. Things They Asked When They Were Small 103
60. The CME 104
61. Paris 106
62. Everything Passes 107
63. The Small Lake among the Trees 110
64. The Circle 111
65. Mad Vlad 6 113
66. After the Pandemic 115
67. Somewhere 116
68. Mad Vlad 7 118

1. Most of All

When I'm happy,
You make me laugh.
When I'm sad,
You make me laugh.
When it's really good,
You make me laugh.
When it's really bad,
You make me laugh.

Ever sitting here with you,
Never leaving your side.
Why would I?
You make me laugh.

Yes, you're sexy, gorgeous,
Clever, talented,
But most of all,
You make me laugh.

2. Loneliness

Sometimes I get lonely.
There, I've said it.
Stiff upper lip,
Never show weakness,
But I've said it.

Being alone is fine.
I'm perfectly happy in my own company,
Comfortable in my own skin,
But what's the point
Without anyone to share it all with?

So yes, I get lonely.
There was a girl I loved,
But she was so young,
I was too old,
Which was tough.

I loved her so much
But I never told her,
I thought she'd run a mile.
But now she's gone; it's my greatest regret,
And I would give anything

To bathe again in her radiant smile.
I'm happy enough being alone,
But maybe not all the bloody time.
It's taken me so long to understand
That loneliness is not a crime.

3. I Confess

Our ending was my confession
That I was too selfish, too unkind.
She wanted to be my sole obsession
But I had other things in mind.

And other women too.
She wanted to be the only one,
My stars, moonstruck, my sun.
But I had others, one or two.

Or three or four,
Maybe more,
Monogamy wasn't for me.
Maybe one day,
Who knows? We'll see.

4. The Little Kick

Oranges, apples, very good,
So nutritious, perfect food.
Ugh! What's this? Broccoli? Yuk!
Ah, strawberries. I'm in luck.

I can hear you, Mummy,
Though you can't hear me yet.
Ah, that deeper voice again:
"Dada? Is that you?"
I won't forget.

Mmm. Tuna again. Fish.
My favourite. Delish.
More dopamine, please,
And serotonin to release
My greatest wish.
How I love this dish.

Ooh! Mozart, did you say?
That's divine.
I'd like to make his music mine.
One day, maybe, in time.

Shouting! That's a bit LOUD!
You woke me up,
Not allowed!

I'm crying with you, Mummy,
Cheer up.
I'm laughing with you, Mummy.
Oh, the cup of joy,
A joyful cup.

A massage, that's new,
Keep rubbing, that's sick.
Let me reward you
With a little kick.

5. My Loss

He said things he never meant
And left unsaid
The things he meant to say.

Her favourite colour was red,
His was green.
So much left unsaid,
So much of her unseen.

No one to fight with now.
No arguments.
No fight left in him.

How he never brushed
Her long, dark hair,
And never will.

How he never put one hand
On her heart
And the other on his
To see if they really did
Beat as one.

Never again to walk in the sun
Or together in the pouring rain,
Or brave the windswept hill
Just for fun.
Never again.

Never admitted the pain
Of her loss
Or got across
How much it hurt.
His world no longer revolving
Around her.
His world no longer revolving.

6. Things I Like

Things I like the most:
Hot buttered toast,
Stories about a ghost,
In a book engrossed,
Sunday afternoon roast,
Being a generous host,
People who don't boast,
Living near the coast,
A funny social media post,
Still surviving in post!
Not hanging off a lamppost,
And not getting dosed,
But being almost always early, poste
Haste.
To feel my innermost
And not to be grossed
Out.
Oh, and Arsenal gaining the most
Points and winning the league!

Fast trains and long-haul flights,
Sunny days and love-filled nights,
Lazy days on the beach,

Forests of oak and beech,
Ash, elm and other trees
Canopies rustling in the breeze.
The other side of the pillow,
The shade of a weeping willow.
Making love beneath the stars,
And wondering if there could be life on Mars.

7. Gratitude

Grateful to wake another day,
Lucky to have what I have,
Lucky to see what I see,
Happy just to be.

Anything is possible.
Be humble.
Life is transitory;
what you have now
may be gone tomorrow.
Nothing lasts forever,
All is change,
Change is all.

8. Millie

Your smile.
The way your mouth moves
When you talk.
Your legs.
And how your bum wiggles
When you walk.
And how you get the giggles.

I make you laugh.
Is that enough?

Well, it's a start,
To win your heart.
My only goal:
Your golden soul.

Our souls are old
And yours is gold,
Your soul survives
From previous lives.

Our worlds collide,
Our souls divide

Then re-unite
To re-ignite.

Out of sight
Of human eye
But we know why
The eagles fly.

Like them we soar
Above the cloud,
How I adore
Our love avowed.

So have we found
Our heaven on earth?
Our love unbound
And filled with mirth.

You make me laugh
And that's enough.

9. Birth of My First Child

The end of sleep
And the end of money
No more spontaneity.
But the start of true love
And the beginning
Of meaning.

10. My Second Child

I've got a baby boy,
He's my claim to fame.
He's a happy little chappie,
He gurgles; he chortles,
He can say my name,
And laughs when I change
His stinky nappy.

11. The Lament of Growing Older

I think I know more than ever,
But my body is just beginning to fall apart.
I know we don't stay young forever,
Wish I'd known that from the start.

If only I'd understood back then
What I realise now,
That time controls you, and that is when
We simply carry on somehow.

That thing older people told you
When you were oh so young,
It was true.
Time gets shorter
As you approach the setting sun.

12. Grey

Grey now.
Grey clouds fill grey skies.
Grey clothes, no brightly-coloured dyes.
Grey soul, grey heart,
Grey memories, no new start.

Where are the bright sun's rays?
Where the blue skies of younger days?
My misspent youth I so enjoyed,
Now all is grey, all hope destroyed.

A grey sea, a grey sea shore,
Where is the gilded youth of yore?
Grey walls, a grey closed door,
Where is she that I adore?

Black. Black. All is black.
She is gone, no coming back.
They all said it wouldn't last.
They were right, she is the past.

13. To a Teenage Son

I'll pick you up
At the gate
At ten past eight.
No time to wait,
So don't be late,
As that would grate
And I'll get irate.
He turned up at 8.25!

14. Blond

You dye your hair
A glorious blond.
Of the other colours
I'm not so fond.

The purple is okay,
Less so the green,
And that black, whole Gothic look
Is best left unseen.

Pink!
Have you had a drink?
I think
It's a bit loud
But that's allowed
Like a sunset cloud.

You don't like your natural colour.
You call it mousey brown
And say it's duller,
But I really like it.
Don't give me that frown.
Okay, okay blond is best,
Forget the rest.

15. Trumpety Trump (With Apologies to Nellie)

Fat little Donald packed his bags
And headed off to the White House
Off he went with a trumpety trump,
Trump, Trump, Trump.

Fat little Donald wore his red tie
As he headed out of the Oval,
Off he went with a trumpety trump,
Trump, Trump, Trump.

Donnie realised the game was up
And faded into history.
Off he went with a trumpety trump,
Trump.
Goodbye,
Trump.
Bye bye,
Trump.

Fat little Donald was bang to rights
And headed off to the jailhouse.
Off he went with a trumpety trump,
Trump, Trump, Trump. Sad!

16. Spam

My spam tells me I'm American.
No, I am not!
I need Medicare
And "auto insurance".
In fact, every find of insurance
Or it's a risk, a dangerous dare.

I need a job.
Plenty of recommendations
Just for me.
But you see
I already have a bloody job.

Do I need to write my will?
Have I updated my CV?
Yes, thanks, everything to the kids still,
And, thanks again, my CV was free.

I'd like a Russian wife
Or a Ukrainian girl in my life.
They don't do irony, do they?
But I apparently suffer
From erectile disfunction

So no use to any kind of wife.
If I can't get it up,
They'd have been sold a pup.

No, I do not want compensation
For an accident I never had,
But if it's any consolation
That makes me very glad.

So many of you want to give me 100 dollars!
If only they existed, I could retire,
But your gift is a lie
And your lies are dire.

Thank you for pointing out
I'm probably a bit overweight.
But a diet? Without a doubt,
Starving myself can wait.

Nigeria! A million you say!
Okay, my friend, let's play.
Send it in used fifties, please do,
A sack full or two should do.
Bank account details?
I don't entirely trust banks,
But I'm sure I can trust you.

Invest in Bitcoin? Cryptocurrency,
Blockchain technology?

Worth how much?
I'm all for being revolutionary,
But sorry, I failed
To get on board. For me,
That ship has sailed.

I have enough credit cards,
But thank you for the chance.
Yes, I'd love to take your survey,
But just a glance
Told me life's too short.

Now I really don't want to appear rude,
But I absolutely do not want to see you nude.

17. They Shall Not Grow Old

I may be becoming old.
If I may be so bold,
Behold:
I'm more controlled,
A stranglehold,
Emotions on hold.

I've been bought and sold,
And resold
Untold times,
Or so I'm told.
I would never fold,
Never withhold
My true feelings.
But I've been bowled
Over by the gold
In human hearts.
Rolled with the punches,
I've extolled
And cajoled
Manifold times.

I had a soldier uncle, Leopold,

Who patrolled
Twofold
But never threefold.
It was foretold.
He enlisted, enrolled,
Couldn't withhold
But had to uphold
The honour of the family name.

He did not grow old.

18. My Girl

Adored
Beautiful
Caring
Delicious
Elegant
Fabulous
Giving
Hilarious
Infectious
Juicy
Kind
Loving
Maternal
Natural
Open
Perfect
Quirky
Radiant
Sexy
Tactile
Unmatched
Vivacious
Winsome

X-rated
Young
Zany.

19. Tonight

We loved by candlelight
All night
It felt so right
Our mutual delight.
She was such a sight
And me, I personified might.
She said, "Well, quite,"
But
I was her knight
In shining armour, white.

I'd accepted her invite,
It seemed only polite,
Her room, the perfect site.
Our passions ignite,
Arousal excite,
Incite, despite
Her lofty height:
6' 4": All right!
She burning bright,
A passage of rite.
She was so tight
And black as night.

But
I had to catch my morning flight
Not out of mind, just out of sight.

20. Great Ball of Fire

The universe is dark.
Black.
Night.
Our daytime
Is only due
To our ball of fire
Giving us light.

Cold.
The universe is cold.
Way, way below freezing.
Lifeless cold.
Our warmth
Is only due
To our ball of fire
Which is so old.

Life.
The universe has no other life
So far as we know.
Lifeless.
Our life
Is only due

To our ball of fire.
All of life.

Love.
Where in the universe
Is love?
That we have love
Is only due to our ball of fire
So far above.

Our world, our planet, our Earth
Our tiny, precious oasis of life
Surrounded by a void
Of cold, dark death
And only due to
Our ball of fire.

Our tiny world it seems
Fits perfectly our little dreams,
But way beyond
More balls of fire
To create new life
And inspire.

21. She

Eyes that see only good
Ears that hear only music
A mouth that speaks only truth
A heart that forgives.
A mind that remembers only the best
Feet that walk towards the light
Hands that create beauty
Arms that embrace with love.
A soul that lives in hope
Faith that binds not divides
Words that soothe not hurt
Dreams that reach for the stars.

22. Loss

Growing older,
And loss
Becomes our overwhelming experience.

But from that experience
Comes a deeper understanding
Of what it is
To be alive,
To be human.

And from that sense of loss,
Of friends, of lovers,
Of our past selves
Comes a deeper appreciation
Of true happiness.

Impossible in transient youth.

23. Actions Not Words

Have you noticed how people
Who say, "I am kind",
Or "I am very tolerant",
Are usually the opposite?
And how those who really are kind,
Who really are tolerant,
Just get on with it?
They never tell us how kind they are,
They don't need to tell us they're tolerant
Knowing that actions
Speak so much louder than words.

24. I Love You More than Anyone

When she said,
"I love you more than anyone else in the world,"
Did she mean,
I love you more than I love anyone else
Or
I love you more than anyone else loves you?
Or maybe both?

25. Mad Vlad 4

Hitler. Stalin. Putin.
Grozny. Unspeakable.
Aleppo. Another war crime.
Ukraine. How did that go?

Stalingard became Volgograd,
Lenngrad returned to St. Petersburg.
Putingrad?
Vlad, baby,
It ain't going to happen.

See you in The Hague.

(Mad Vlad, Mad Vlad 2 and Mad Vlad 3 are in *"No Words and Other Poems"*)

26. What It Takes

It takes
Absence to appreciate presence,
Ignorance to realise knowledge,
Disbelief to grasp faith,
Noise to enjoy silence,
Isolation to accept company,
Loneliness to love people,
Dullness to learn imagination,
Misery to know happiness,
Coldness to perceive warmth,
Rejection to achieve acceptance,
Stupidity to assimilate wisdom,
Failure to recognise success,
Loss to osmose to triumph,
Fear to embrace freedom,
War to comprehend peace,
Indifference to cherish love.

27. The Soundtrack of My Life

Sure, The Beatles, The Stones and The Who,
Ray Davies, Hendrix, Pink Floyd and Cream,
The music tracks that helped us dream.
Bowie, Dylan, Springsteen, Marley and The Dead,
Mozart, Chopin, Bach and Beethoven.
Music, music, enough said.
But
Engines.

Engines in cars, engines in planes,
Engines in bikes, engines in trains,
Burning fossil fuels,
See how Clarkson drools
While our planet groans.
And tree-hugging eco-warrior moans.
Burning petrol, burning coal,
Destroying the Amazon
And the human soul.

28. She Is Gone (12 January 2023)

She is gone.
There is no more poetry to write.
No more poetry. Full stop.
My muse.
The girl with the golden heart
And the beautiful soul.

She is gone.
My ray of sunshine,
Our hope, our joy.
Mauled by a pack of frenzied dogs,
But which dogs? And why?
Unimaginable. Incomprehensible.

Tearing her beautiful,
translucent flesh.

An eye witness:
Her shouting,
The dogs growling.
No barking, just growling.
Then screaming.
The dogs growling.
Then whimpering.

The growling dogs.
Then silence.

The lethal attack concluded.
Silence.
And blood.
Blood.
And silence.

Looks of a supermodel,
Heart of an angel.
So wise beyond her years,
And so observant, didn't miss a thing.
Why can nothing stop these tears?
Why won't the birds sing?

Nothing means anything any more.
That's not entirely true
But that's how it feels.
The light has gone out.
Still so much to live for,
But so much less.

I used to see her every day,
The highlight of my day.
Used to.
She won't be here tomorrow,
Or the day after.
Or ever again.

29. Rivers

Enoch Powell said, "Rivers of Blood."
We say rivers of rosehips,
Rivers of orchids,
Rivers of jasmine,
Rivers of peace and love.

Virgil said, "The Tiber.
Will foam with much blood".
We say rivers of salmon,
Rivers of rainbow trout,
Rivers of sole,
Rivers of peace and love.

Unger said,
"The blood of the generals
is gonna flow
like the rivers of ancient Babylon"
We say rivers of light,
Rivers of hope,
Rivers of faith,
Rivers of peace and love.

30. Another Year

January, I'm in the library,
Too cold to venture out.
When it warms up, someone shout.

February, still being literary,
Dark and wet,
Not venturing out yet.

March, the needles of the hybrid larch,
Greening, sharp, heralding spring.
The March birds sing.

April, the rain a trickle,
Then the eponymous showers,
And blooming of the flowers.

May, when we say
The darling buds are here to stay.
Don't ever go away.

June, get here soon,
Beneath the sparkling stars,
And silvery moon.

July, and no more school,
Time to be children,
And play the fool.

August, the month of fun,
Splash in the water,
Bask in the sun.

September, and we remember
That summer feeling,
Autumn invading.

October, not quite sober,
The month I was born,
Each birthday a new dawn.

November, so much colder,
The dying ember,
The year so much older.

December, solstice, Saturnalia,
And how we cheer
Another year.

31. Divorce

Learning to walk again,
One step at a time,
Left, right, left, right.

Trying to remember to breathe,
One breath at a time,
In, out, in, out.

Struggling to talk again,
One word at a time,
Noun, verb, noun, verb.

Opening my eyes to see again,
One sight at a time,
Open, blink, open, blink.

Training my ears to hear again,
One sound at a time,
Loud, soft, loud, soft.

Learning to feel again,
One emotion at a time,
Pain, loss, pain, loss.

Learning to love again.
No, not that.
Not yet.

32. Two Degrees

Two degrees, it feels much colder,
Another birthday, ten years older,
The weight of the world
On my shoulder,
Like a boulder.

Another year,
Wiser and bolder,
But I never told her
How I longed to hold her,
And never consoled her.

Beauty, eye beholder.
The unknown soldier.
How I smoulder.
A secret decoder.

I should have phoned her.

33. Action Now!

When things are getting you down,
When it all seems too much,
Remember
We are a pimple
On the backside
Of the universe,
A grain of sand
On the vast beach
of the Cosmos.

It's just a few thousand years
Since our great, great, etc., grandfathers
Were hunting with spears,
Since our great, great, etc., grandmothers
Gave birth without pain relief, only tears.

Only two hundred years ago
No modern medicines,
Or dentistry.
Ouch!

We are the lucky ones,
The freedom generation,
Our daughters and sons

In an age of instant gratification.

There was no nuclear war,
It remained cold,
But there is climate change,
And we must be bold.

We must take the action needed,
Greta and Al must not go unheeded,
We're running short of time
To prevent this global crime.

34. By Sunlight

On the twenty-fifth floor,
In the sky,
I was at her door.
We both knew why.

And so, for years
We loved
Without tears,
By sunlight, by candlelight,
By moonlight, by starlight.

I can still taste her lips,
Kissed without a care,
I can still see the wind
In her golden hair,
I can still feel her breast
On my ribs as she walked beside me,
By sunlight, by candlelight,
By moonlight, by starlight.

We were like Gods, the very best,
And I, foolishly, thought we'd pass every test,
By sunlight, by candlelight,
By moonlight, by starlight.

35. My Trouble 'n' Strife

My perfect little squeeze,
Gorgeous small avian boat,
Her minces, huge blue windows,
Her Hampsteads sparkling white.
Her north and south, smoochy delicious,
Beautiful little fireman's,
Long blond barnet, swanlike Gregory,
Pretty little tobies.
Her small but strong brass bands,
With slender, sensitive bell ringers.
Cute little Bristols,
Such a sexy fife and drum,
Her stunning Kyber pass,
The way she wiggles her bottle and glass.
Her willowy pins,
Her lovely, rounded biscuits,
Above her tiny, perfect plates,
With pretty little Bromleys.
Oh, and her jack 'n' Danny,
Her Morris. Wow!

Met her down the battle,
My local rub-a-dub.

I'd spotted her through the Tommy,
Nursing a Vera and tonic.
She was with her China,
I was on my Jack,
I'd been having a good, long butchers.
Her China, a bubble, had too much bunny
So, when she went to the khazi,
We grabbed our weasels
And scarpered sharpish.
Had a few sherbets,
We had a giraffe,
Got a bit Brahms 'n',
Well, elephants,
And all for less than a pony.

Next day, called her on the dog,
We went for a Ruby.
I wore my best whistle,
She said I was her treacle.
We did it in my jam jar,
She left me cream crackered!

And all these years down the frog,
She's never told me porkies,
Never caused me any Barney,
Would you Adam and Eve it?

36. The Decision

A fork in the forest,
Which way the prettiest?
Which the safest?
Which to take?
The decision to make.
Both inviting, but both with a thorn,
And neither well worn.

A sliding doors moment,
which would I lament?
Which might I regret?
What would each beget?

A moment of sliding doors
On holiday in the Azores,
Which one sinks, which one soars?
There were no tours
Or books to guide,
And nowhere to hide.

In the bright early morning light,
I made my choice,
But in the early hours of the night,

Which was the Rolls Royce?
Which was right?

And on that strange and fateful morn,
Did I make a choice forlorn?
It was a blur, I felt a stir:
Her, not her.
She, not she.
And so it came to be.

37. Khovanskoye

Moscow's largest cemetery,
The biggest in Europe.
Two million square metres.
All those graves,
All that grief and bereavement.
Row upon row.
Stone angels,
Snow, flowers and wreaths,
Photographs of the dead
Half-buried in white,
As far as the eye can see,
Stretching to the horizon.
Each with its own story,
A life well-lived, or not.
And beyond,
Space for more,
For more grief and bereavement.

38. The Lady in the Lake

Her ankles were bound.
She was gagged.
Hands tied behind her back,
Drowned.
"Gruesome,"
the police pathologist said.
No sword.

39. Holidays

Christmas.
"Don't talk to your mother like that."
"Do NOT talk to your mother like that."
"Who do you think you are?"
"Who the HELL do you think you are?"

"Don't talk to your father like that."
"How dare you?"
"How dare you!"
"HOW DARE YOU!"

"Oh, shut up."
"No, you shut up."
"No, YOU shut up."
"STFU."

"Just stop it."
"Stop it."
"Stop it."
"Stop it!"

"Make it stop."
"God, make it stop."

40. Maybe

Maybe
One day
We will grow up
And replace
'Long to reign over us'
with
'Land of hope and glory
Mother of the free'.
Or maybe not.

41. My Friend's Wife

My lesbian friend calls her partner
Her wife,
Her trouble and strife,
And my friend's partner calls my friend
Her wife.

But that word, 'Wife,'
If not implying subjugation,
Maybe some kind of subordination?

She needs a new word,
A word less absurd
Than 'wife'
To describe
The love of her life.

'Partner?' But they're married.
'Spouse?' Ugly word.
'My love?' Beloved?
'My forever love?'
'My better self?'
'The better part of me?'
'My forever union?'
Maybe just stick with 'wife.'

42. Peering through the Tears

Sitting at the top of the stairs,
Trying to be as small as possible,
Trying to be invisible.

Downstairs:
CRASH! SMASH!
Saucepans flying, crockery smashing,
Shouting and screaming.
They never swore,
So that made it all right?
Not like us,
We swear all day and all night.

A door slams.
BANG!
He'd gone into another room.
He was never violent.
Never.
But door-slamming
Was his specialty.
Her's was throwing things.

Creeping slowly,

So slowly,
Downstairs.
Scurrying to the kitchen,
Sees his mother,
Sobbing at the sink.

It must be his fault.
He must work harder at school.
He must get better at sports.
He must be more polite.
It must be all his fault.

43. Attention Span of This Generation

All the world's a stage.
My kids say I'm showing my age.
Shakespeare is strictly for the old.
They know nothing.

It requires more than ten seconds of attention.
Great art requires powers of retention.
Anyway, why bother reading a book? Just Google it.
They are wrong.

Theatre? Not as good as a film or a video game.
I mean, no CGI, it's so lame.
But look, it's live, happening now right before your eyes.
They are clueless.

Opera? Don't be so utterly absurd.
Fat singers, foreign language, don't understand a word.
Now this I get, an acquired taste.
But they lack the patience.

Classical music? Beethoven? Mozart?
They appreciate that it's great art

But it goes on for 'way too long'.
They prefer a three-minute, three-chord pop song.

Cricket? Five days to play a test?
Five days? Give it a rest!
FIVE DAYS for just one match?
Bang! Goal! 1-0.

Relationships? You're having a laugh.
No, I don't need to find my 'other half',
It's far too much like hard work.
They may have a point.

44. Humans

We have the technology,
The knowledge and the intellect
To save our planet,
To feed the poor,
To eradicate disease,
To end all war.

And yet.
And yet we still continue
To destroy ourselves and our home,
We cannot get beyond
Thousands of years
Of human stupid.

I fear for my children
And their children.
Wars. Climate Change.
Man-made.
MAN-MADE.

"He behaved like an animal,"
When things go bad so people say.
That attitude is abysmal,

Animals do not behave that way.

Other animals don't stab you in the back,
Commit mass murder, torture on the rack.
They are just as capable of sympathy, empathy,
Love and feeling pain
As the ape with the super-sized brain.

Acts of terror, genocides,
Sadism, killing for fun.
I am no misanthrope,
 I try to see the good in everyone,
But animals don't behave that way.
Humans do.

45. New Love

I love you so much.
I can't think beyond that line.
How I wish that you were mine.
I'd do anything for you,
Anything you want me to.

I love you so much.
I long to tell you.
I can't tell you.
You'd run a mile.
Wouldn't see you for dust.

46. To My Ex

I know the blame was mine,
But it was your's too.
I still love you, you know it's true,
But I just can't take being with you.

We had this love, oh so 'sublime',
Which slowly disappeared with time.
The light went out in your eyes,
Extinguished by all your lies.

Yes, I still love you,
But I'm not in love with you.
We didn't talk enough,
We never saw it through.

A memory that has faded
Of a love that became jaded.
No more second chances,
No more lovestruck glances.

I went from being 'my beautiful man',
To the 'evil spawn of Satan'!
How do we learn, how can we gain,
Never to make the same mistakes again?

Look, I'm sorry I ruined your life,
That you were so unhappy being my wife,
Playing a part which didn't suit you.
I could have helped if only I knew.

47. Larry

Dog!
A dog in my house!
That PM was a louse.
Yapping nonstop
And that was just the dog.
Bloody stinking
Pooh everywhere.
What were they thinking?

Some fat policy advisor picked me up.
Big mistake.
I messed him up, scratched him very hard,
He yelped, fat tub of lard.

That other PM, strumming his guitar,
Very relaxed, he went too far.
Tried so hard to be my friend,
When will this human nonsense ever end?

The one who threw his phone around,
Got so angry, a roaring sound.
Some of them found him rather scary
But I was cool, I'm Larry, and I'm lairy.

That woman who was here and gone

In, what, forty days?
She promised she would get things done
But seemed to live in a permanent daze.

Plenty of mice, very nice,
And rats, not the human kind.
The rodents spread like lice
Until they meet me, and I unwind.

48. A Homily

Keep lawyers and bankers away,
Keep naysayers at bay,
And advertising men,
And used car salesmen.

Words that matter are softly spoken, or read,
Not shouted in unrest.
Don't use cruel words,
 They can't ever be unsaid.
Silence is often best.

Forgive your enemies,
They won't know what to do.
Forget those who trespass against you.

Every road you take has potholes,
Traps to make you fall,
Often hidden.
Don't worry,
Troubles come when bidden.
Bide your time, it conquers all,
Until they're gone.

Try to keep up with the news.
Have opinions and views,

But learn when to keep them
to yourself.

Don't sermonize
But harmonise
Practice what you preach,
By your actions teach.

Good judgement
Comes with time,
From the mistakes you make.
Learn from them,
There's much at stake.

Live a good and decent life,
Find yourself a good wife,
So when you're old and grey,
You can live again each day.

Sometimes you win,
But sometimes you lose.
Take it on the chin.
Lay off the booze.

Live simply,
Give kindly,
Care deeply,
And love without limit.

49. Red Red lights (To the Tune of Red Red Wine)

Red, red lights
On my way home,
Angry verbal fights,
Bumper-to-bumper chrome.

I'll be late, dinner burnt,
Dogs in need of a walk,
Same lesson, never learnt,
Wife in need of a talk.

Red, red lights,
Everyday,
Ruin my life
In the same way.

Wife will moan, angry face,
Will this nightmare never end?
"Take the train," my disgrace,
Drives her round the bloody bend.

Red, red lights,
Oh my word,
Famous Black Rod,
Men in tights.

On my way from SW One,
Rain, rain, no sign of the sun.
I work hard, need the pay,
Same old traffic every day.

Red, red lights,
Please change to green.
I'm bang to rights,
This is obscene.

It's like they're stuck,
An eternity of red,
Just want to get home
to my marital bed.

Red, red lights,
Ruining my nights,
Making me late again,
Twisting my fate again.

50. The Whether Fourcast

Today will be wry and funny,
Later, a chance of some pain.
Tomorrow, slow over high terrain,
Further south, a land of milk and honey.

By next Sunday,
Het and hindy
In Rawalpindi,
Wry again by Monday.

Brace yourselves, it might start wailing,
And prepare yourselves for a storm of sheet,
If you're driving, you'll feel like you're sailing,
Best to stay in, keep off the street.

Next week, back to funny, happy to inform,
Get down to the peach, temperatures rising,
Life's a beach, back to the seasonal norm,
Chill the Riesling, nothing surprising.

The long-range forecast is better by far.
Yes, you can get back in your car.
You can drive a country mile,
Free at last, so smile.

51. The End?

The end of all mankind,
Of all recorded and unrecorded time,
The eyes' light fading humankind
A universal power no longer sublime.

And in the church, we lit another candle,
Contemplated the holy, unholy dread,
We took that candlestick by the handle
And smashed the life out. Dead.

The word of God, your god, not mine,
In temple, mosque, synagogue church,
Art and love will not confine,
But blindly on and on we lurch.

To the light from the dark,
In waking as in sleep,
Clear sight where the wet dogs bark,
To mark the shallow from the deep.

So we, as humankind, must not forget
Our mission to spread and carry love.
We may not have reached the stars just yet,

To both sides, as below, as above.

But at our planet's gasping last breath,
My beautiful homeland, so pleasant and green,
Ours and every species' final death,
Its beauty may one day be unseen.

Our planet is old, but we are not,
Our lifespan short, a few hundred thousand years,
One day, the species time forgot,
Let's not end it all in tears.

52. At the Supermarket

"NO, we can't go yet,"
The kid stared at his mum.
"I can't take much more of this shit,"
He murmured under his breath, mumbled.
In the next aisle, an infant throwing a hissy fit.

Meat and poultry, not today.
Sugar and cakes, no way.
A stroll around "Household essentials,"
Time to flex my DIY credentials.

English cheese, yes please.
Anything other than row and rows
Of bloody cheddar?
Put it in the shredder.
I want Wensleydale, Cheshire,
Red Leicester,
But all they had was
Cheddar, cheddar, cheddar.

Soft drinks and booze:
Which wine to choose?

That wino looks confused,
Guess he's been abused.

Fresh fruit, a great display,
A bunch of ripe bananas.
Why is that woman
Still wearing her pyjamas?

Careful with that trolley!
Nearly crashed, what folly.
No, not my fault,
Hey, almost an assault!
Act your bloody age!
I bet you give good road rage.

Pharmacy, final stop.
Need some toothpaste
And a razor, smooth-faced.
Smile at the pharmacist, two-faced,
Does he have a suggestion
For this painful indigestion?

Checkout time,
The queue was fine
Until
"This checkout is now closed
please join another line."

Pack my bags? OK my friend,

Let's keep you in employment,
Hope you're enduring this deployment.
Same reason I don't use the automatic machines,
Still behind their pandemic screens.

53. Growing Old

All that get up and go
Has been and gone.

All that Va Va Voom
Has met its doom.

All that cut and thrust
Has turned to rust.

All that blind ambition,
Those hopes of sedition.

All that makes the will bend
Has met its end.

All that virile seed
Dried up, no more need.

All that sowing of wild oats
Forgotten, all those Shakespeare quotes.

All that talk of a fresh start
Reduced to an old man's fart.

All those dreams of a bright tomorrow
Reduced to this most profound sorrow.

54. The Funeral

What are these words?
They are absurd.
She's lying in that wooden box.
Can't speak through the tears,
Can't manage a single word.

I tried to feel something,
Anything.
Not sad,
Celebrating her life
But it cut like a knife.
All those condolences
They drove me mad.

And when it finally hit
Like a twitching, foaming fit,
A billion shattered fragments
Of a million broken dreams.
She has really gone it seems,
It seems inconceivable.
Unbelievable. Unimaginable.

Spiralling down and further down

Nothing and no one could rescue him,
Certainly not that dreadful hymn.
Nothing and no one could save him.
Nothing.
No one.
Ever.

55. Never Mind

I went upstairs to do I know not what,
Because once I got there I forgot.
What on Earth I'd gone there for,
So went back down to the lower floor.

I talk to myself all the time,
In couplets, with words that rhyme.
I can just about remember my name
But nothing else remains the same.

Then I again retraced my steps,
These moments that so perplex.
My addled brain,
So disorientated,
It's like I'm permanently sedated.

It can't have been important, never mind,
I'm like the blind leading the blind.
Oh yes! I know! Oh no, it's gone,
Not worth wasting any more time on.

I'm tired now, stifling a yawn,
Insomniac, it'll soon be dawn.

"Am I a good man or a fraud?
Have I loved a good life? Tell me, Lord."

Yes, hedging my bets on the religion thing,
I used to play and dance, and sing.
Now I'm focused on whatever comes next,
Trying to find some meaning and context.

The years erode us so,
That's all I really know.
And now I need the loo!
Older reader: Is this you too?

Though after a lifetime of mockery, denial and rejection
Not sure the Supreme Being will give me a warm reception

56. I Bought Them a Puppy

Why me
To clean up
Your wee?
What about
My kids
Whose dog
You're supposed to be?

Why me
To clean up
Your poo?
What about
My kids
Who
Made me buy you?

Please grow up fast,
Get bigger soon
Or I might not even last
This afternoon.

Yes, you're fun,
Your high-pitched howl,

A bundle of energy
But, really, I am done.
Your bladder and bowel!
There is no synergy.

My living room floor,
The stench is obscene,
Get out of that door
Into the garden green.

What did I do
Apart from buying you
For them?
Why condemn me
To cleaning up
After the bowel and bladder
Of this little pup?

57. Mad Vlad 5

Hail Tsar Vlad!
Stark raving mad.
Genocidal barbarian,
Homicidal authoritarian.

Not quite hyperborean,
An arse holothurian,
Perhaps your Praetorian
Guard will send you to a Siberian
Gulag.

You are not Shakespearean,
But the antithesis of humanitarian,
You should be in a sanitarium.
It's one thing to be a disciplinarian,
Another to be a fascist totalitarian
And murderer of Syrian
children.

Such a sad little man,
That sad little boy
With the inferiority complex.
Do you ever have unpaid for sex?

Your grandfather, the cook
To Lenin and the murderous Joe.
Like him, you brook
No dissent.
Up through the KGB,
And so you came to be
Head of State.
But nothing will ever wipe your slate
clean.

Think to the future, not the past,
Time to pay the ferryman.
Time to be gone, hideous half-man,
Say your goodbyes, nothing can last
Forever.
Except your condemnation,
Eternal damnation.

58. Hey Kids!

Do not mock me when I seek
Your help with tech: I am no geek!
Born before computers were so everyday,
And mobile phones were still years away.
Remember:
I changed your nappies,
I helped you take your first steps,
I taught you to feed yourselves,
I offered you unconditional love
And I still do.

59. Things They Asked When They Were Small

What is a dream?
Why do I have an Adam's Apple?
Why don't I have one too?
Why is the sky blue?
Why is grass green?
Why is the Moon round?
How many stars are there in the sky?
Will the Sun last forever?
Where do people go after they die?
How does electricity work?
What is gas?
Why did you just call me a gasbag?
Why can't dogs talk?
Can goldfish smell their food?
Do Africans live in mud huts?
Why is Mummy drunk again?
Can I get drunk when I'm older?
And the killer:
Daddy, why do you smoke?

60. The CME

It exploded, our affair,
Like a blazing solar flare,
Hit us like a geomagnetic storm
With the power to reform and transform
Both our lives.

But then,
Became a Coronal Mass Ejection,
A CME to herald our rejection,
Catastrophic, cataclysmic,
All our love spent,
An extinction event
For our love.

Travelling at two million miles per hour,
To smash, consume, devour
The lasting traces,
Worn out places
Of our love.

Its force is spent, let's not lament
The past, it's done, its race is run.
But now another wants to take me to the Sun,

And tell me when the time has come
To love again.

61. Paris

City of light, grey in the rain,
Nature's douche on the banks of the Seine.
Concorde, Place of the guillotine,
Powdered, sightly, but slightly obscene.

Your scarlet lips and scented hair,
How you move your hips, your face so fair,
The Eiffel Tower, the Moulin Rouge,
Your reputation huge despite this deluge.

And, of course, the food and wine.
I want to make each menu mine.
If I lived inside of you,
I'd grow so fat.
She laughed.
"Amen to that."

62. Everything Passes

You can lose but still win,
You can win but still fail,
You can fail but still succeed,
You can succeed but still fall short,
You can fall short but still prevail,
You can prevail but still fall flat,
You can fall flat but still rise up,
You can rise up but still go down,
You can do down but still soar again,
You can soar again but still break down,
You can break down but still rise again,
You can rise again but still recede,
You can recede but still triumph,
You can triumph but still surrender,
You can surrender but still win the battle,
You can win the battle but still lose the war,
You can lose the war but still vanquish,
You can vanquish but still languish,
You can languish but still conquer,
You can conquer but still decline,
You can decline but still prosper,
You can prosper but still back the wrong horse,
You can back the wrong horse but still overcome,

You can overcome but still run aground,
You can run aground but still keep going,
You can keep going but still flounder,
You can flounder but still hit the target,
You can hit the target but still miss the point,
You can miss the point but still achieve,
You can achieve but still deteriorate,
You can deteriorate but still ascend,
You can ascend but still descend,
You can descend but still climb the mountain,
You can climb the mountain but still go downhill,
You can go downhill but still excel,
You can excel but still flop,
You can flop but still flourish,
You can flourish and still hit the skids,
You can hit the skids but still thrive,
You can thrive but still fold,
You can fold but still profit,
You can profit but still miss the boat,
You can miss the boat but still outwit
You can outwit but still be ruined,
You can be ruined but still compete,
You can compete but still be found wanting,
You can be found wanting but still defeat,
You can defeat but still fly,
You can fly but still dive,
You can dive but still float,
You can float but still sink,
You can sink but still possess,

You can possess but still yield,
You can yield but still gain,
You can gain but still be in vain,
You can be in vain but still be happy,
You can be happy but still be sad,
You can be sad but still surpass,
You can surpass but still come to nothing.

63. The Small Lake among the Trees

The calm water is saying,
Slow down, take your time,
Reflect.

The leaves, rustling in the gentle wind
Want us to meditate, contemplate,
Serenity

The water lilies, their flowers blooming,
Opening to the sky, the World,
The Sun.

But we,
We must return to the cacophony
Of the modern, tuneless symphony,
Our restless lives.

64. The Circle

I stumble in a circle,
A rut of faults and habits,
Never corrected, never improved,
Never moved on.
Just deeply grooved,
My heart unmoved
By yours or any other song.

Inside my head, round and around,
My breathing is the only sound.
But you, breathless, now no more,
Your brooding absence still so raw,
Its presence red in tooth and claw.

So where do we go
When we can't break free?
What's the point if we are so
Stuck in this circle for eternity?

Around and around and around,
Unbroken circle, no new ground,
Just aimless stumbling, without meaning,
Lost all sense of overweening.

Dreaming, yes,
Teeming with dreams,
but this circle unending
Is never what it seems.

65. Mad Vlad 6

Hey Vlad,
Looking sad,
Pale, ill, yellow skin,
Is it gout or gangrene,
Jaundice or sin?

Hey Vlad,
Barking mad,
Ukraine just won't knuckle under,
You made an enormous blunder.

Hey Vlad,
They were bad,
I see your angry frown:
Your generals let you down.

Hey Vlad,
I'm so glad,
You look forlorn,
I could have sworn
I saw you shudder
In fear,
Oh dear,

You've lost your rudder.

Hey Vlad,
Felicidad!
I saw you tremble,
Now you resemble
A cornered beast
As they queue to feast
On your still warm corpse.
Too bad, Vlad.

66. After the Pandemic

They had found him.
He'd been dead for some time.
The smell was appalling.
He had starved to death,
Surrounded
By dozens of rolls
Of toilet paper.

67. Somewhere

Somewhere, a baby is being born,
Elsewhere, someone else is dying.
Somewhere, someone is singing,
Elsewhere, someone cannot even speak.
Somewhere, someone is marvelling at nature,
Elsewhere, someone else is blind.
Somewhere, someone is listening to Mozart,
Elsewhere, someone else is deaf.
Somewhere, someone is running,
Elsewhere, someone cannot even walk.
Somewhere, lion cubs are being born
Elsewhere, a lion is being shot by scum for 'sport'.
Somewhere, someone is taking his health for granted,
Elsewhere, someone else is dying of cancer.
Somewhere, someone is a billionaire,
Elsewhere, someone is desperately counting the pennies.
Somewhere, someone is stuffing his face,
Elsewhere, a child is dying from malnutrition.
Somewhere, someone is showing off his collection of cars,
Elsewhere, a child is walking miles to school.
Somewhere, someone is enjoying another drink,

Elsewhere, someone is dying of liver failure.
Somewhere, someone is pampering their pet dog,
Elsewhere, a street dog is being killed for food.
Somewhere, someone is basking in the sun,
Elsewhere, someone is dying in the drought.
Somewhere, someone is dancing in the rain,
Elsewhere, someone is drowning in the flood.
Somewhere, someone is living in a time of peace,
Elsewhere, someone is fleeing the men with machetes.
Somewhere, someone is drinking his fill,
Elsewhere, the rivers have all dried up.
Somewhere, someone is moaning about Monday morning
Elsewhere, someone is dying without warning.
Somewhere, someone is complaining that they're cold,
Elsewhere, more polar ice is melting.
Somewhere, someone is gazing in wonder at the stars.
Elsewhere, someone is gazing in wonder at the stars.

68. Mad Vlad 7

Hey Mad Vlad!
Mister one gonad!
You compared yourself
To Peter the Great.
I have to say
That really did grate.

The greatest of the Tsars understood
Russia's future lay with the West,
Believing his country's legacy would
Be secured and the rest,
As they say,
Would be history.

He left his legacy,
Modern, scientific, the Enlightenment,
While you will leave only a travesty
And the widow's lament.

At the river Neva he built
Mother Russia's greatest city.
You? Well, you have built nothing
Except a nation's guilt.

Like a colossus
The Bronze Horseman,
A man of consequence.
While you, a homicidal little man,
Are as nothing, as dust,
Despite your temporary dominance.

He could be ruthless, see Bulavin,
But also showed mercy, unlike Stalin
Or that monster Vladimir Putin.
He let better counsel hold sway
But you, little man, just run away.

Your weakness is now cruelly exposed
As rival warlords vie for power,
Wallowing in blood as you bulldozed
Your proud but smaller neighbour, unbowed.
If you were here, you'd be in The Tower.

The centre cannot hold much longer,
You'll leave your country weaker, not stronger.
Now you're trying to deny Ukraine
Even its food, it's precious grain.

Your very own Holodomor,
Imitate your hero Joe,
You're just a blood-soaked dinosaur,
Another genocidal maniac.

You came cheap, off the rack,
Another murderous lunatic
With your pathetic little prawn-dick.
Go howl at the moon
And, please, die soon.

Slava Ukraini!

Epilogue: for Natasha: Sonnet 18